Discover! 5

T0288641

Homes Around the World

Jacqueline Martin

Contents

OXFORD
UNIVERSITY PRESS

OXFORD
UNIVERSITY PRESS

Great Clarendon Street, Oxford OX2 6DP

Oxford University Press is a department of the University of Oxford. It furthers the University's objective of excellence in research, scholarship, and education by publishing worldwide in

Oxford New York

Auckland Cape Town Dar es Salaam Hong Kong Karachi Kuala Lumpur Madrid Melbourne Mexico City Nairobi New Delhi Shanghai Taipei Toronto

With offices in

Argentina Austria Brazil Chile Czech Republic France Greece Guatemala Hungary Italy Japan Poland Portugal Singapore South Korea Switzerland Thailand Turkey Ukraine Vietnam

OXFORD and OXFORD ENGLISH are registered trade marks of Oxford University Press in the UK and in certain other countries

ISBN: 978 0 19 464497 6

An Audio Pack containing this book and an Audio download is also available,
ISBN: 978 0 19 402222 4

This book is also available as an e-Book,
ISBN: 978 0 19 464731 1.

An accompanying Activity Book is also available
ISBN: 978 0 19 464507 2

Printed in China

This book is printed on paper from certified and well-managed sources.

ACKNOWLEDGEMENTS

Illustrations by: Roger at KJA Artists pp4 (cave people), 5 (straw hut); Alan Rowe pp36, 37, 40, 42; Martin Sanders/Beehive Illustration pp12, 40 (map); Gary Swift pp14, 16.

The publisher would like to thank the following for their kind permission to reproduce photographs and other copyright material: Alamy Images pp3 (Yurt house, Mongolia/Imagestate Media Partners Limited - Impact Photos), 5 (Tulor ancient village, Chile/Megapress), 9 (White house/Stock Connection Distribution), 11 (Tin city, South Africa/John Crum), 16 (Yurt house, Mongolia/Imagestate Media Partners Limited - Impact Photos), 17 (Floating Village Catba Island, Vietnam/dbimages), 21 (Buckingham Palace, London/Mark Richardson), 21 (Windsor Castle, England/Jon Arnold Images Ltd), 27 (Casa Batllo at night, Barcelona, Spain/Art Kowalsky), 29 (Civilian houses in Fujian, China/View Stock), 30 (Rwanda Orphanage School/Jenny Matthews), 32 (Strawbale house/Camera Lucida); British Museum Images p5 (Terracotta model house/The Trustees of the British Museum); Bruno Bellec p26 (Reflection of Mineral/Atelier Tekuto); Corbis pp10 (Vimanmek Teak Mansion/Jean-Pierre Lescourret), 25 (Building made of cans/Roger Ressmeyer); Getty Images pp12 (Detached country house/Oliver Beamish), 25 (House made out of plastic bottles/AFP), 31 (Eldoret, Kenya/Christian Science Monitor), 34 (Girl watching TV screens/John Eder); iStockphoto pp3 (Taos/John Woodworth), 6 (Machu Picchu, Peru/Jamo Gonzalez Zarraonandia), 18 (Monument Valley/Steven Allan), 28 (Taos/John Woodworth); Lonely Planet Images pp3 (Hi-rise residential apartments/Ricard l'Anson), 8 (Hi-rise residential apartments/Ricard l'Anson), 8 (Gabled buildings, Amsterdam/Thomas Winz); National Geographic Image Collection pp3 (Stilt house, Cambodia/Michael S. Yamashita), 15 (Stilt house, Cambodia/Michael S. Yamashita); Nordic Photos pp3 (Mountain cottage, Switzerland/Pictor), 13 (Mountain cottage, Switzerland/Pictor); OUP pp4 (Cave drawings/Photodisc), 4 (Pyramids, Egypt/Digital Vision), 4 (Great Wall of China/Photodisc), 5 (Parthenon/Photodisc), 5 (Colosseum, Rome/Photodisc), 5 (Machu Picchu/Photodisc), 35 (Space Station illustration/Photodisc); Photolibrary pp6 (Paldalmun gate, Hwaseong Fortress, South Korea/Jose Fuste Raga), 14 (Berber mud house, Morocco/Alan Keohane), 17 (Reed Island, Titacaca Lake, Peru/JTB Photo), 23 (Topkapi Palace, Istanbul/San Rostro), 24 (Troglodyte houses, Spain/Brigitte Merle), 27 (Pennsylvania, USA/Peter Cook), 33 (row of sod-covered houses/Kristian Maack); PunchStock p19 (Couple cooking food over campfire/Pixland); Robert Harding World Imagery pp3 (Thatched cottage/Ellen Rooney), 9 (Thatched cottage/Ellen Rooney), 18 (Horse-drawn gypsy caravan/Roy Rainford), 20 (Zijin Cheng, The Forbidden City Palace Museum, Beijing/Chris Kober), 22 (The White House, Washington D.C/Jonathan Hodson), 26 (Toraja houses and granaries, Indonesia/R H Productions), 29 (Aerial view of Yanomami, Brazil/Robin Tenison); Shutterstock p7 (Ancient Chinese houses/July Flower).

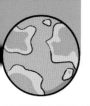

Introduction

The place where we live, sleep, and eat is called our home. There are lots of different types of home. Homes around the world are made of many different materials, and can be many different shapes and sizes.

How many different types of home can you think of?
What types of home do you have in your country?
What are they made of? How old are they?
What are the homes below called?
Where in the world can you find these homes?

Now read and discover more about homes around the world!

Homes in the Past

About 50,000 years ago people lived in caves. Then about 5,000 years ago people started to build homes. People in the past didn't have homes like we have today. How were these homes different?

Caves

Caves were dark and didn't have windows. They protected people from bad weather and wild animals. The doors were made from animal skins. There was no kitchen or bathroom. Cave people cooked their food on fires.

In hot weather they didn't live in homes at all – they lived and slept outside.

In some places where there were no natural caves, people had to dig caves out of the hills.

50,000 years ago
Cave people

5,000 years ago
Ancient Egyptians

3,400 years ago
Ancient Chinese

Straw and Mud Houses

The first houses were made from dry plants like straw. These houses weren't very strong.

The Ancient Egyptians built houses with bricks made of mud and straw. They put the mixture into molds and left them in the sun to dry. Then they built walls with the bricks and put wet mud on top. There were holes in the walls for windows and doors. Egyptian houses had flat roofs. People often slept on the roof because it was nice and cool.

In the past other people in Asia, Africa, and South and North America built mud houses, too. Different-colored mud made different-colored bricks!

Mud Houses, Chile

2,400 years ago
Ancient Greeks

2,000 years ago
Ancient Romans

600 years ago
Incas

Today

Stone Houses

Some people in the past built houses from stone because it was strong. Poor people lived in small houses with only one room. Important rich people built stone castles to live in. These took many years to build.

The Ancient Greeks built houses with mud bricks on top of stone blocks. The roofs were usually made of tiles.

The Incas lived in Peru. They built houses with stone blocks. Each block was carefully cut and polished so the houses looked great when they were finished. The houses had thatched roofs made of straw.

Machu Picchu, Peru

Discover!

Inca walls were strong because there were spaces between the blocks. When there was an earthquake, the blocks moved, but the walls didn't fall down!

Wooden Houses

The Ancient Chinese people built wooden houses. They had long roofs made of a wood called bamboo. Many Chinese houses were built on platforms to protect the wood from water.

The Ancient Romans built houses with wood, mud, and stone. They also used some materials that we use today, like concrete. Some Roman houses had a bathroom, plumbing, and heating.

A Wooden House, China

Go to pages 36–37 for activities.

Homes Today

Some people today live in homes made of natural materials like mud, stone, or wood. Many people live in homes made of man-made materials like concrete, bricks, plastic, and glass. What is your home made of?

Homes in the City

In big cities many people live in apartments. These are homes on one floor of a bigger building. Some apartments are above shops or in old houses. Others are in tall buildings called skyscrapers. Apartments are often built on top of each other in one building because there isn't enough land for a lot of houses.

Some houses in towns are built together in a row. These are called row houses, or terraced houses. They are narrow so you can build many on one street.

Other Homes

Outside the city there is more land for homes. People often have gardens or land to grow vegetables. Some people live in big houses detached from each other. Detached houses have space all around them.

Other people live in houses called bungalows, or ranch houses. These are detached houses with all the rooms on one floor.

The old building below is called a cottage. It is made of bricks and has a thatched roof. People in many parts of the world build homes with thatched roofs.

Homes for Rich People

Rich people sometimes live in big houses called mansions. They have electricity, running water, central heating, air conditioning, nice bathrooms, expensive furniture, carpets, and sometimes even swimming pools! They often have big gardens, too.

The mansion below is in Thailand. It is made of a wood called teak. A natural oil in the wood protects it from the weather and insects. Teak is very good for building houses and furniture.

Homes for Poor People

Poor people often don't have enough money to buy or build their own home. Some families share small apartments with other families. The whole family sleeps in one room, and two or three families share one bathroom.

Some very poor people can't live with other families, so they have to build homes with things that other people throw away, like bits of metal, fabric, or wood. Places where there are lots of these homes together are called shanty towns. There's no electricity or running water.

Many people today are homeless and do not have a home at all. Homeless people sometimes sleep on the street in big cities. In some places there are shelters where they can stay, but sometimes the only thing they have is a cardboard box!

→ Go to pages 38–39 for activities.

3 Different Climates

The climate is different in different parts of the world. People build different homes depending on the climate. What type of climate do you have in your country?

Climates
- polar (cold)
- temperate (mild)
- tropical (hot and wet)
- desert (dry)
- mountainous (cold)

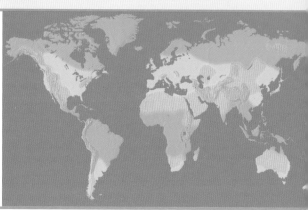

Temperate Climates

In temperate climates the weather is usually mild. Homes are often built with bricks. Bricks keep water out and keep the homes dry. Homes often have large windows to let the sun in, and a chimney so people can light a fire when it's cold. Where it rains a lot, people build houses with sloping roofs so that all the water runs off and doesn't get into their houses.

Cold Climates

In cold mountainous climates homes are often built with stone. If forests grow there, wood is also used. The lower walls of this chalet are built with stone because it is strong. This helps the chalet to stay up if there's an avalanche. The upper walls are built with wood because wood keeps the heat in. These homes have long sloping roofs so that heavy snow falls off.

Some people, like the Inuit people in the Arctic, even build their winter homes with snow. These homes are called igloos. Snow walls keep the wind out and make it quite warm inside. Some large igloos have five or six rooms and more than 20 people live in them.

A Mountain Chalet

Hot Desert Climates

In hot deserts the temperature is very hot in the day and cold at night. People need homes that protect them from sun, heat, wind, and cold. Where there aren't many trees or rocks, people build houses with mud and grass. The houses have small windows to keep the sun out. This makes the house cool, but it is dark inside so people spend most of the day outside or on the roof. Thick walls keep the house cool in the day and warm at night. They also protect the house from the strong desert winds.

Discover!

In some deserts it's so hot that people make homes underground because it's cooler there.

Tropical Climates

In tropical climates the weather is hot and wet. People need homes to protect them from sun, wind, and rain. Lots of forests grow here and the people use the trees to make wooden houses. Mud bricks would break!

There are often floods in tropical climates, so people build houses on stilts. The stilts keep the house cool and protect it from snakes and water! Long roofs provide shade, and wooden shutters on the windows keep the sun out.

A House on Stilts

Go to pages 40–41 for activities.

Homes that Move

Most homes stay in one place, but some people travel and take their home with them. Can you think of any homes that can move?

A *Ger*, Mongolia

Tent Homes

Nomads look after animals and move their homes when their animals need fresh grass to eat. They live in tents that can be folded up and carried. Many people in Mongolia are nomads. They travel around with their animals and live in tents called *gers*.

In summer some Inuit people in the Arctic live in tents made from deer skins and whale bones.

Discover!

Some Native Americans lived in tents called teepees. These tents were made from animal skins.

Homes that Float

Lots of people in the world live on houseboats. People sleep, cook, eat, and sometimes work on them. Some houseboats are used as floating shops, so you don't have to get to land to buy food!

Some people live on canal boats. These boats are long and narrow, so that they can travel along narrow rivers or canals. About 200 years ago these boats carried materials for big industries, but today the boats are used as homes.

The Uros people in Peru make floating houses from the plants that grow in the lake. First they make a floating island for the house to stand on and then they make a house, all from plants!

Floating Houses, Peru

17

Homes with Wheels

About 150 years ago in North America some people lived in wagons. The wagons were pulled by oxen. People traveled around looking for new places to live. At night they slept in the wagon or outside on mats.

Today some groups of people still live in wagons and travel around looking for work. Their wagons are usually pulled by horses.

Modern wagons are called travel trailers, or caravans, and they are usually pulled by cars.

Some people drive motor homes, or RVs. These are like a big car or van that you can live in. Many people like to drive in these on vacation because they can travel to lots of different places and see the countryside. You don't need to sleep outside caravans or RVs. The seats and tables change into beds at night!

Vacation Homes

Many people like to go camping. They sleep in tents and cook their food outside on a fire.

Some people have two homes – one home for the winter and one for the summer – and they move between them. The home doesn't move, but the people do!

Go to pages 42–43 for activities.

5 Famous Homes

There are lots of famous people in the world. Some of their homes are quite famous, too. Can you think of any famous homes in your country?

The Forbidden City

The Forbidden City in Beijing in China is a big palace. There are palace gardens and nearly 1,000 buildings. It is the largest ancient palace in the world. It took 15 years to build and it is surrounded by a high wall and a moat. For 500 years it was the winter home of the emperors of China. In summer they moved to the summer palace 12 kilometers away. Today the Forbidden City is a museum.

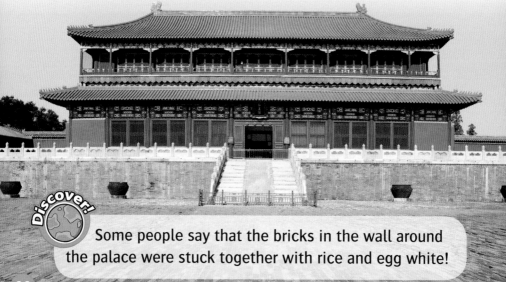

Discover! Some people say that the bricks in the wall around the palace were stuck together with rice and egg white!

Homes for a Queen

The Queen of the United Kingdom has two homes. When she is in London she lives in Buckingham Palace. Part of the palace is now an art gallery and you can also visit the gardens.

The Queen's main home is Windsor Castle. It is one of the largest castles in the world. Many kings and queens are buried here. In November 1992 there was a big fire at the castle. It took 15 hours and a lot of water to put out the fire. The fire destroyed a big part of the castle, but most of it has been built again.

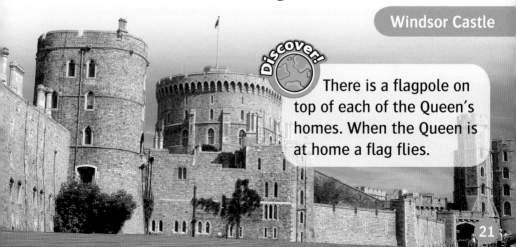

Windsor Castle

Discover! There is a flagpole on top of each of the Queen's homes. When the Queen is at home a flag flies.

21

The White House

The White House is in the USA. It is the home of the American president. The first White House was built in 1800, and 43 presidents have lived here – that's all the presidents except for the first president, George Washington. About 5,000 people visit the White House every day!

The White House today has:

6 floors	147 windows	1 bowling alley
132 rooms	28 fireplaces	1 movie theater
412 doors	35 bathrooms	1 jogging track
3 elevators	1 tennis court	1 swimming pool

Topkapi Palace

Topkapi Palace is in Istanbul in Turkey. It was the home of the sultans. Up to 4,000 people lived in the palace. There were schools, shops, libraries, gardens, and other buildings, so the people who lived there never had to go out! Some parts of the palace were destroyed by fires and earthquakes, but you can visit the other parts because there is a museum.

Discover!

About 800 people worked in the palace kitchens and they cooked about 6,000 meals every day!

Go to pages 44–45 for activities.

6 Unusual Homes

Most homes around the world have four walls and a roof and they are built with bricks, stone, mud, wood, or concrete. Some people live in more unusual places. Would you like to live in any of these homes?

Rock Homes

Some people still live in caves! The strong rock walls protect them from all types of weather. Cave homes can be very comfortable today, and they usually have windows and electricity.

Almost half of the people who live in Guadix in Spain live underground in caves. Many of the homes have chimneys, but these aren't to let smoke out – they are to let air in! These homes have water and electricity, and many have televisions and Internet connections.

Unusual Materials

Some people make homes out of unusual materials. The house above is in New Mexico in the USA. Its walls are made of mud, car tires, and cans! The people who live here didn't use these materials because they had nothing else to use – they wanted their house to look different!

The woman below lives in El Salvador in Central America. She built her house from plastic bottles because she didn't have enough money for bricks! It took nearly two months to collect all the bottles and three months to build the house.

Unusual Shapes

Some people live in homes that are unusual shapes. Sometimes their homes look like other things. Sometimes there is a reason for the unusual shape. This house in Japan looks like a diamond, and it has a parking space for the car!

The first people who came to live in Toraja in Indonesia came in boats. There is a story that a big storm damaged their boats so they couldn't float. The people then used the boats as roofs for their houses. Now they still build houses with roofs shaped like boats!

Designer Homes

Architects sometimes design homes to look different. Sometimes they copy things from nature. Can you think of any famous architects? What famous designer homes are there in your country?

The house on the right is in Spain. It was designed by Antonio Gaudí.

The house below is in the USA. It was designed by Frank Lloyd Wright and is built over a waterfall. You can hear the waterfall from every room!

Go to pages 46–47 for activities.

Homes for Everyone

Some people in the world live alone. Other people live with their families, other families, or with friends. Who lives with you?

Family Homes

In big towns each family often has its own small home, but in many places in the world lots of generations of a family often live together. This can be helpful because the grandparents can look after the children while the parents work. Sometimes lots of different families live together in the same building, but on different floors.

The people who live in this house in Mexico use ladders to get between floors. On summer nights they often sleep on the roof like the Ancient Egyptians did. It's cool and it doesn't rain very often.

Community Homes

This house is in China. It's called a *tulou*. It's a big round house, three or four floors high, and it's made of mud. There is only one door and all the main windows are inside so it is well protected. Lots of families live here, sometimes up to 800 people! Each family has two or three rooms. The house is plain on the outside, but the inside is often brightly decorated.

The Yanomami people live in the Amazon rainforest in South America. In each village, everybody lives together in a big round home called a *yano*. It's built with wooden poles and a thatched roof made from leaves. There aren't any walls. Up to 400 people live here. Each family has its own area where they have hammocks to sleep in.

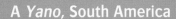

A *Yano*, South America

29

Other Homes

In Europe, North America, and Australia most people live in homes built for one family. Old people often live in a separate home. Sometimes they live near their families, but sometimes they are far away. Some old people live in an old people's home with lots of other people. They can talk, play games, and keep each other company when they can't see their families.

Children with no parents are called orphans. If they have no other family to look after them, they can live together in a big home called an orphanage.

An Orphanage School, Rwanda

Living without a Home

Some people's homes are destroyed by hurricanes, earthquakes, floods, or wars. People then live together in refugee camps and they all try to help each other. Sometimes people have to live here for many years.

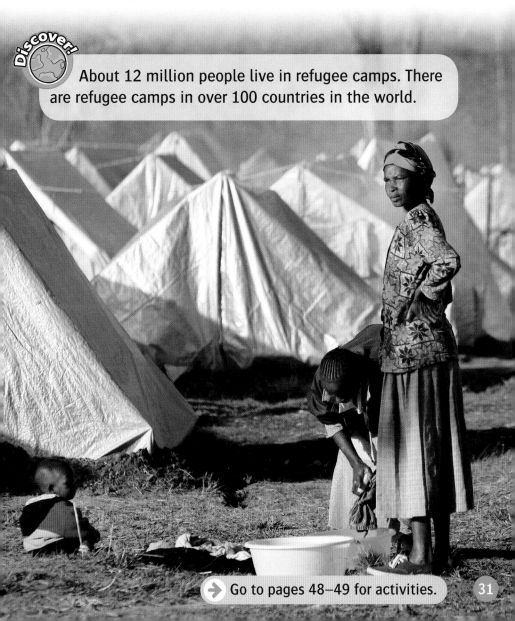

Discover!

About 12 million people live in refugee camps. There are refugee camps in over 100 countries in the world.

Go to pages 48–49 for activities.

8 Future Homes

About 100 years ago we didn't have flushing toilets, stoves, or central heating. What will we have in our homes in another 100 years?

Eco Homes

People are damaging the environment by using too much coal, oil, and gas for energy. Maybe in the future all homes will be more environmentally friendly and will use clean energy from the sun and the wind.

We can save energy with homes that are insulated to stop energy escaping through roofs, doors, or windows. The house below is made of straw inside. It's warm and environmentally friendly.

These houses in Iceland have roofs covered in grass because grass is a good insulator.

Homes that Protect Us

Our climates are changing and there are more and more hurricanes and floods. How can we protect our homes?

Some new homes have walls made of steel and concrete. They won't fall down in a hurricane. Architects are also designing homes for the future that will float. Scientists are investigating new waterproof materials for homes.

People living in brick houses can die in earthquakes if the houses fall on them. New homes made from cement and foam won't fall down in an earthquake because they are light. They are cheap to make and environmentally friendly.

High-Tech Homes

In the future what technology will homes have? Scientists say that we will be able to use one computer to watch television, look at the Internet, turn the lights on and off, and tell us if there's a burglar in the house! They say that lights will turn on when we walk into a room, and refrigerators will tell us when food is bad to eat! We will be able to talk to other people through an electronic screen and see who's at the front door on our television!

What Next?

Maybe in the future, homes will look quite different from what we see today. What materials do you think we will use to build homes? What shapes will they be? Maybe our homes will make all their own energy. Maybe they will be made of recycled materials.

Maybe we will all live in outer space! What do you think? The International Space Station is like a home in space. It was built in 1998. Astronauts from 16 countries have lived there since it was built.

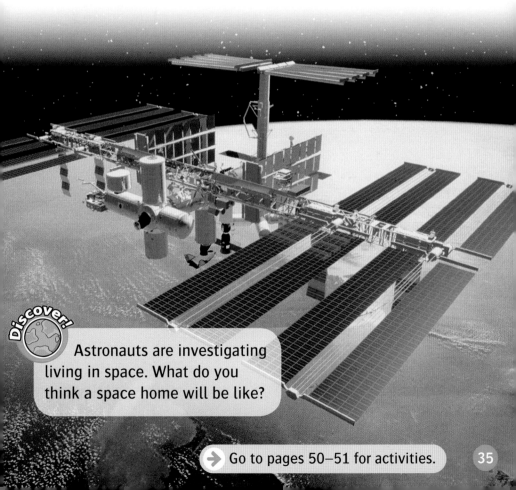

Discover!

Astronauts are investigating living in space. What do you think a space home will be like?

Go to pages 50–51 for activities.

1 Homes in the Past

← Read pages 4–7.

1 Write the words.

> mud house   wooden house   ~~stone house~~
> straw house   cave   castle

1 _stone house_

2 _____

3 _____

4 _____

5 _____

6 _____

2 Write the numbers.

> 5,000   3,400   ~~50,000~~   2,400   2,000

1 About _50,000_ years ago people lived in caves.

2 The Ancient Egyptians built mud houses about _____
years ago.

3 Chinese people built wooden houses about _____
years ago.

4 About _____ years ago the Ancient Greeks built stone
houses.

5 About _____ years ago some Roman houses had heating.

3 Write *true* or *false*.

1 Cave homes had windows.   *false*

2 In summer, cave people slept outside. _____

3 The Incas built houses with stone. _____

4 Ancient Greek houses were built on a platform. _____

5 Ancient Egyptian houses had thatched roofs. _____

6 Ancient Chinese houses had plumbing. _____

4 **Match. Then write the sentences in order.**

a   b

| e | Leave holes for windows and doors. |

| | Build a wall. |

c

| | Put the mixture into molds. |

d

| | Leave the molds in the sun. |

| | Put wet mud on the wall. |

e

| | Mix mud and straw. |

f

How to make bricks from mud and straw:

1 Mix mud and straw.

2 _____

3 _____

4 _____

5 _____

6 _____

② Homes Today

← Read pages 8–11.

1 Write the words. Then complete the diagram.

> terraced houses   skyscraper   bungalow
> detached house   cottage

1 an old building with a thatched roof _____

2 houses built together in a row _____

3 a very tall building _____

4 a detached house with rooms on one floor _____

5 a house with space all around it _____

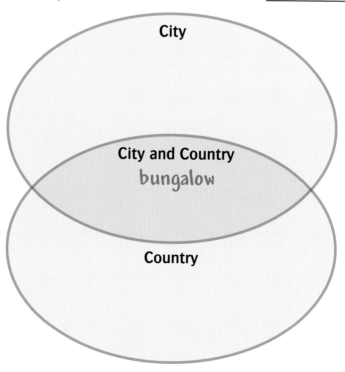

City

City and Country
bungalow

Country

2 Write *true* or *false*.

1 Houses in a row are called apartments. _____

2 People without homes are called homeless. _____

3 Poor people live in mansions. _____

4 Bungalows are all on one floor. _____

5 Homes in the city often have gardens. _____

6 Terraced houses have space all around. _____

7 Cottages have thatched roofs. _____

8 Rich people live in shanty towns. _____

3 Write sentences with these words.

rich   terraced   country   detached   skyscrapers

1 Houses in a row are called _____

2 _____

3 _____

4 _____

5 _____

4 Where do you live? Write about your home.

_____

_____

_____

_____

_____

③ Different Climates

← Read pages 12–15.

1 Write the words. Then color the map.

temperate   tropical   ~~polar~~   desert   mountainous

Climates

1 _polar_ = ⬛   2 _____ = ⬛

3 _____ = ⬛   4 _____ = ⬜   5 _____ = ⬛

2 Where do you live? Draw ★ and write the country on the map.

3 Complete the chart.

~~hot~~ wet cold windy sunny mild snowy icy dry	

Polar	Tropical	Desert	Temperate
	hot	hot	

4 Complete the sentences. Then write sentences for the extra words.

~~hot~~ stone cold wet snow mild
underground floods chalet stilts

1 In ___hot___ places people sometimes live underground.

2 Igloos are made of _____ .

3 In temperate climates the weather is _____ .

4 Homes in the mountains are often made of _____ .

5 In hot deserts it is _____ at night.

6 In tropical climates it is hot and _____ .

7 There are often _____ in tropical climates.

8 In some deserts people build their homes _____ .

9 _____

10 _____

4 Homes that Move

← Read pages 16–19.

1 Write *boat, wagon,* or *tent*.

1 a home that floats   <u>boat</u>

2 a home on wheels   _____

3 a home that's made from animal skins   _____

4 travelers live in this   _____

5 nomads live in this   _____

6 a car or a horse can pull this   _____

7 a home on a canal   _____

2 Circle the correct words.

1 wagon / (tent)

2 motor home / wagon

3 canal boat / houseboat

4 wagon / motor home

3 Order the words.

1 made /are / Teepees / skins. / from / animal

<u>Teepees are made from animal skins.</u>

2 shops. / houseboats / are / floating / Some

_____

3 thin. / long / boats / and / are / Canal

_____

4 by / Wagons / pulled / oxen. / were

_____

5 to / people / like / Many / go / camping.

_____

6 people / make / The / Uros / houses. / floating

_____

4 Answer the questions.

1 Why do nomads move their homes?

_____

2 Why are canal boats long and thin?

_____

3 What are wagons pulled by today?

_____

4 What do people do when they go camping?

_____

5 Famous Homes

← Read pages 20–23.

1 Find and write the words.

jmthewhitehouseitopkapipalacenctheforbiddencityyflwindsorcastlehj

1 The White House
2 _____
3 _____
4 _____

2 Match. Then write the sentences.

The Queen of the United Kingdom	the USA.
In November 1992 there was	is in Beijing.
The White House is in	has two homes.
43 presidents have lived	15 years to build.
The Forbidden City	a fire at Windsor Castle.
The Forbidden City took	in the White House.

1 The Queen of the United Kingdom has two homes.
2 _____
3 _____
4 _____
5 _____
6 _____

3 Write ✓ or ✗. Then write sentences.

	Buckingham Palace	The White House	Topkapi Palace	The Forbidden City
high walls	✗	✗	✗	✓
gardens				
museum				
art gallery				
moat				
movie theater				
flag				
swimming pool				

1 The Forbidden City has high walls.

2 _____

3 _____

4 _____

5 _____

6 _____

7 _____

8 _____

6 Unusual Homes

← Read pages 24–27.

1 Complete the chart.

~~mud~~
concrete
wood
glass
stone
bottles
cans
plastic
bricks

Natural	Man-Made
mud	

2 Correct the sentences.

1 Cave homes today are very (uncomfortable.)

  <u>Cave homes today are very comfortable.</u>

2 The cave homes in Guadix have chimneys to let smoke out.

  _____

3 Cave homes today don't have Internet connections.

  _____

4 The Toraja houses have roofs shaped like cars.

  _____

5 Architects sometimes copy things from books.

  _____

3 **Find and write the words from pages 24–27.**

1 four things that cave homes have today

_____   _____

_____   _____

2 four unusual building materials

_____   _____

_____   _____

3 two famous architects

_____   _____

4 four countries

_____   _____

_____   _____

4 **Which unusual home do you prefer? Why?**

_____

_____

_____

_____

_____

_____

_____

_____

_____

7 Homes for Everyone

← Read pages 28–31.

1 Write the words.

refugee camp   orphanage   *tulou*   old people's home

1 This is a home for children with no parents. _____

2 Old people can live together here. _____

3 People can live here when their homes are destroyed.

_____

4 This is a big round house. _____

2 Order the words.

1 live / old / Some / people / families. / their / near

_____

2 *tulou* / mud. / A / made / is / of

_____

3 doesn't / any / *yano* / have / walls. / A

_____

4 orphans. / parents / with / called / Children / are / no

_____

5 destroyed / Some / are / homes / people's / floods. / by

_____

6 live / million / in / 12 / About / camps. / people / refugee

_____

3 Write the numbers.

> 800   400   3 or 4   2 or 3   0   1

1 The number of rooms each family has in a *tulou* is _____ .

2 Up to _____ people live in a *tulou*.

3 Up to _____ people live in a *yano*.

4 The number of floors in a *tulou* is _____ .

5 The number of doors on a *tulou* is _____ .

6 The number of walls on a *yano* is _____ .

4 Answer the questions.

1 Where can people who have lost their home live?

_____

2 What can old people do in an old people's home?

_____

3 Why is it helpful for grandparents to live with families?

_____

4 What is the roof of a *yano* made from?

_____

5 Where do people sleep in a *yano*?

_____

6 What is an orphanage?

_____

8 Future Homes

← Read pages 32–35.

1 Complete the puzzle. Then write the secret word.

1 Straw houses are environmentally ___ .
2 Clean energy comes from the ___ .
3 In the future we will see who is at our door on our ___ .
4 Our ___ will tell us when our food is bad.
5 Scientists are investigating ___ materials.
6 Houses made from steel and ___ won't fall down in a hurricane.
7 We can save ___ by insulating our homes.
8 Using too much coal, oil, and gas ___ our environment.
9 Maybe in the future we will live in ___ !
10 Clean energy also comes from the ___ .
11 In the future a ___ will tell us if there's a burglar in the house.

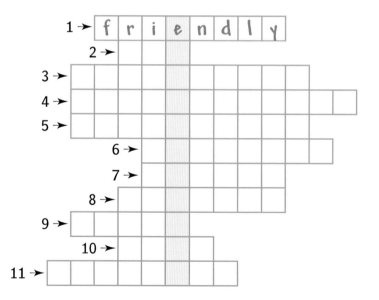

1 → f r i e n d l y

The secret word is:

2 Circle the correct words.

1 Architects have designed houses that will **fly** / **float**.

2 Using coal is **bad** / **good** for the environment.

3 Clean energy comes from the sun and the **windows** / **wind**.

4 Straw houses are **cold** / **warm**.

5 **Foam** / **Brick** houses can fall down in earthquakes.

6 Foam houses are **expensive** / **cheap** to make.

3 Write about homes in the future. What will they look like? What will they be made of?

_____

_____

_____

_____

_____

_____

_____

_____

_____

_____

_____

_____

A Homes Survey

1 Draw a plan of your home and your street.

2 Do a survey of homes in your area.
How many different types are there?
What are they made of? How old are they?

What type of home is it?	What's it made of?	How old is it?

3 Make a summary to show your results. Display your results.

An Unusual Home

1 **Design an unusual home. First make notes.**

What shape is it?

_____

What is it made of?

_____

Does it have stairs, windows, doors, walls, a roof?

_____

How many rooms does it have?

_____

What are the rooms used for?

_____

How is it decorated?

_____

Why is it unusual?

_____

2 **Draw your home and write about it. Display your design.**

Glossary

air conditioning something that cools the air in a building

alone without any other people

ancient from thousands of years in the past

art gallery a museum for art

avalanche a lot of snow that falls down a mountain

block something that is a rectangle with flat sides

bone the hard part of a skeleton

brick a man-made building material that is a rectangle with flat sides

bright strong and easy to see (for colors)

burglar someone who steals things

bury to put a dead person into the ground

canal it is man-made and like a river

cardboard very thick paper; boxes are made of this

carry to take something to another place

cement a building material that sticks bricks together

central heating it keeps your house warm with hot air or water in pipes

cheap not expensive

chimney it's on the roof of a building; smoke goes through it

climate the type of weather in a country

coal it's hard and black, and you can burn it to make fire

comfortable nice to be in, for example, soft beds or chairs

community all the people who live in a particular place

concrete a building material made of cement, sand, stones, and water

countryside the land outside a town or city

damage to make something bad or weak

decorate to make something look nice; to put things on it

deer a wild animal

destroy to damage something very badly

die to stop living

dig to make a hole in the ground

earthquake when the ground shakes

electricity a type of energy

elevator (*or* **lift**) it carries people up and down a building

emperor a king

energy we need energy to move and grow, and machines need energy to work

environmentally friendly being kind to the environment

escape to get away from something

fabric a soft material

famous known by many people

fire this is produced when something burns; it's very hot

fireplace the place where you make a fire in a house

flag a piece of material with a special design for a country

float to stay on the top of water

flood when there is a lot of water where it is usually dry

foam a soft, light building material

forest a place with a lot of trees

fresh not old (for food)

fridge a machine that keeps food cold

furniture things in a house, for example, a sofa or a bed

gas it's not a solid or a liquid; it's used for cooking

generation grandparents, parents, and children are different generations of a family

glass a hard material; you can make windows and bottles with it

grass a green plant

hammock a type of bed

heat something that is hot; to make something hot

hole a space in something

homeless when you don't have a home

hurricane a very strong wind

industry the production of things, especially from factories

insect a very small animal with six legs

insulate to use a material to keep something warm

investigate to find out about something

island a piece of land with water all around

keep company to be with somebody so they are not alone

keep in to stop something going out

keep out to stop something going in

lake a big area of water

land the part of Earth that is not water

lower the bottom part

main the largest or most important

man-made made by people; not natural

mat a small, thin piece of material that you put on the floor

material what things are made of

meal breakfast, lunch, and dinner are meals

metal it's hard and made from minerals

moat the water that goes around a castle

mold (or **mould**) you put mud and straw into it to make a brick

mud wet soil

narrow thin

natural comes from nature; not made by people

nature all plants, animals, and things that are not made by people

oil a liquid from plants or animals that we use for cooking

outer space where the moon and stars are

ox (plural **oxen**) an animal like a cow

past many years ago

plain not decorated

plastic a hard, man-made material

platform a flat area higher than the ground

plumbing the pipes that carry water to homes

pole a thick, circular piece of wood

poor not rich

protect to keep safe from danger

provide to give

recycle to use again

rock a very hard, natural material

roof the top part of a building

row objects in a line

RV a recreational vehicle

screen the front of a computer or television

seat something to sit on

shade somewhere not sunny

shutter you put it on the outside of a window

skin the part of an animal that covers the outside of the body

sloping not flat

smoke it comes from a fire

snake an animal with a thin body and no legs

space an area where there is nothing (see also **outer space**)

steel a strong, hard metal

stilts wooden poles

stone a very hard, natural material

storm bad weather; lots of wind and rain

stuck held together

sultan a king

surround to be all around something

technology the design of new machines

thatched grass or plants tied together to make a roof

tile a small piece of hard material used to make a roof

tire (or **tyre**) the thick, soft ring on a wheel

upper the top part

war when people or countries fight

waterproof can keep water out

wheel a round object that makes cars and bicycles move

Oxford Read and Discover

Series Editor: Hazel Geatches • CLIL Adviser: John Clegg

Oxford Read and Discover graded readers are at six levels, for students from age 6 and older. They cover many topics within three subject areas, and support English across the curriculum, or Content and Language Integrated Learning (CLIL).

Available for each reader:
• Audio Pack
• Activity Book

Available for selected readers:
• e-Books

Teaching notes & CLIL guidance: **www.oup.com/elt/teacher/readanddiscover**

Subject Area / Level	The World of Science & Technology	The Natural World	The World of Arts & Social Studies
1 300 headwords	• Eyes • Fruit • Trees • Wheels	• At the Beach • In the Sky • Wild Cats • Young Animals	• Art • Schools
2 450 headwords	• Electricity • Plastic • Sunny and Rainy • Your Body	• Camouflage • Earth • Farms • In the Mountains	• Cities • Jobs
3 600 headwords	• How We Make Products • Sound and Music • Super Structures • Your Five Senses	• Amazing Minibeasts • Animals in the Air • Life in Rainforests • Wonderful Water	• Festivals Around the World • Free Time Around the World
4 750 headwords	• All About Plants • How to Stay Healthy • Machines Then and Now • Why We Recycle	• All About Desert Life • All About Ocean Life • Animals at Night • Incredible Earth	• Animals in Art • Wonders of the Past
5 900 headwords	• Materials to Products • Medicine Then and Now • Transportation Then and Now • Wild Weather	• All About Islands • Animal Life Cycles • Exploring Our World • Great Migrations	• Homes Around the World • Our World in Art
6 1,050 headwords	• Cells and Microbes • Clothes Then and Now • Incredible Energy • Your Amazing Body	• All About Space • Caring for Our Planet • Earth Then and Now • Wonderful Ecosystems	• Food Around the World • Helping Around the World